The Fresh Air Fix™ Survival Guide

How to escape the rat race and reconnect with the great outdoors.

by Juliette Dyke

© 2011, Juliette Dyke, Fresh Air Fix

ISBN: 978-1-4477-5064-2

The right of Juliette Dyke to be identified as author of this work has been asserted by her in accordance with the Copyright, Designs and Patents Act 1988.

All rights reserved. No part of this publication may be reproduced, stored in a retrieval system, or transmitted in any form or by any means, electronic, mechanical, photocopying, recording or otherwise, without either the prior written permission of the author or a licence permitting restricted copying in the United Kingdom issued by the copyright Licensing Agency Ltd, Saffron House, 6-10 Kirby Street, London EC1N 8TS. This book may not be lent, resold, hired out or otherwise disposed of by way of trade in any form of binding or cover other than that in which it is published, without the prior consent of the author.

Design by John Amy at Promo Design
www.promo-design.co.uk

Contents

Spring — 8

Summer — 16

Autumn — 24

Winter — 32

"The need of quiet, the need of air, the need of exercise, the sight of sky and of things growing seem human needs, common to all men". Octavia Hill, a co-founder of the National Trust, 1895

LOVE the great outdoors but live in an urban jungle? Stuck at a desk all day but long to feel the breeze on your face? *The Fresh Air Fix Survival Guide* is here to change all that. In fact, I want to start a Fresh Air Revolution!

More and more of us are living in urban areas, and spending less time outdoors than ever. In fact, according to the National Trust's *Outdoor Nation campaign*, we city dwellers are in danger of becoming disconnected from our countryside and green spaces. The younger generation in particular are growing up to see the outdoors as somewhere unfamiliar and even frightening.

However, the scientific benefits of 'green time' are there for all to see, from reducing stress to preventing illness and even helping you live longer (source: *Natural England*).

Spending time outdoors helps us to feel more relaxed, re-energised and able to appreciate the simpler things like the smell of a campfire or pulling up your first home-grown vegetables. Exercising outdoors saves you money on gym fees, and just enjoying the view of a natural scene instead a bare wall has been shown to reduce anxiety.

The Fresh Air Fix Survival Guide is packed full of tips for squeezing in a bit more outdoor time, whether it's a suggestion for an action packed weekend, or a just few minutes during your lunch hour. It's also divided into seasonal chapters, so you'll be able to dip into each chapter depending on the time of year. However there is no reason why you can't put these suggestions into action whenever you like,

though perhaps only the bravest readers will try a wild swim in the middle of January!

The nerve centre of the Fresh Air Revolution is my blog, *www.freshairfix.com*, where you will find a community of like-minded people and start planning your next big (or little) adventure.

The idea for the blog, which led to the writing of this book, came about as ideas often do, on a dreary Monday morning as I struggled into work. Having spent a glorious weekend of walking in the hills, swimming in the sea and sleeping under the stars, all my stress had melted clean away but I could feel it building up again fast as I faced another week of overcrowded tubes and a hectic office job, where I would sit at desk all day in a building that overlooked… another building.

Friends of mine told me they felt the same way, stifled by office jobs, stuffy commutes and airless gyms, and longing to experience the 'feel good factor' of being active in the great outdoors on a regular basis, not just on holidays or at weekends.

This became the catalyst for me to create an inspiring outdoors blog and community, to help people share ideas on where to go and what to do, and provide a virtual 'fix' of fresh air every single day.

I also wanted to celebrate the Great British outdoors, showing people how many incredible landscapes we have to enjoy right here on our shores, from national parks to incredible beaches, snow capped mountains and rugged coastlines.

I also hoped to demystify the idea of what an 'outdoorsy' type is. You don't have to be ultra fit, or love reading maps, or have a thing for eating freeze dried meals, just leave that to Bear Grylls. Everyone can get out in the fresh air and enjoy some of what beautiful Britain has to offer, and best of all it's completely free!

My aim is to create a ripple effect of change, encouraging more people of every age and background to reconnect with the great outdoors and feel the benefits of having a regular 'fresh air fix'. So let's get started Britain, we've got some mountains to climb!

JULIETTE DYKE

SPRING

Whether you're getting fit, planting some seeds or swapping a four wheeled commute for two, spring is the perfect time to make a fresh start.

Spring

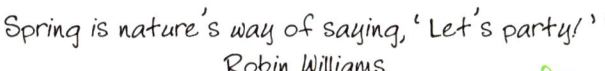

"Spring is nature's way of saying, 'Let's party!'"
Robin Williams

Take the road less travelled by

 The daily commute is a necessary evil for most of us, relying on congested tubes, trains, buses and cars to make the journey. However, you could transform your journey by trying one these outdoor alternatives that are cheaper, greener and possibly even quicker:

Cycling

Cycle commuters are an increasingly familiar sight on our streets, and we all know that it's good for our health and our wallets, but did you know that in rush hour a bike can actually complete the same journey faster than a car? The key is to plan your journey, making best use of side streets and cycle paths. In the capital, TFL have free cycle route maps available from their website, *www.tfl.gov.uk*, helpfully marked to show both the busier and quieter routes.

Walking

You might be surprised by how quickly you can get from one part of a city to another on foot, as well as gaining some invaluable 'me time' before and after work.

Route planning tools like *walkit.com* enable you to check the distance before you set off, or search for suitable routes uploaded by other users. All that's left to do is don some comfortable shoes for the journey (you can always change into smarter ones for work) and set off.

Push power

Bring out the big kid in you with an adult micro scooter, which will raise your heart rate, get you out in the sunshine and is a whole lot more fun than being squashed in a packed tube. Just make sure you don't hunch over and alternate legs to avoid getting rather unevenly developed thighs!

Kayaking

Admittedly, this one might take a bit more planning but the rewards are immense. You need to identify an entry and exit point for your kayak, and be able to store your gear during the day, as well as plan around any tides. Even so, it's completely carbon neutral and allows maximum smug factor as you glide past harassed looking drivers, giving them a friendly wave as you pass.

Ferry

If you live in a town or city on a river, investigate the local ferry and water taxi services. In London, the Thames Clipper service makes the journey from Blackfriars to Canary Wharf in just 18 minutes, and unlike peak time trains, you are allowed to take your bike on board.

Feel the buzz

 How do you normally unwind after a long day at the office; have a glass of wine? Switch on the TV? Or head down to the bottom of the garden to harvest your own honey?

City gardens across the country are increasingly buzzing with activity as urban beekeeping becomes more and more popular. UK beekeeping courses are now regularly oversubscribed and the British Beekeepers' Association (BBKA) reported a 25% jump in membership to 15,000 in 2010, with figures set to keep on rising.

These hives are not all being kept in quaint little country gardens either, far from it. In fact, many urban bee keepers are finding space for their hives on roof tops, down side alleys and in miniscule city gardens. Alison Benjamin, author of *Keeping bees and making honey*, explains what's got her hooked about this hobby.

"I love it because it reconnects you with nature. City life can cut you off from the seasons. Urban beekeeping is also a way of greening cities and improving health by eating locally-produced honey."

City gardens are actually great for bees because of the milder climate and wider variety of plants and flowers, which help sustain them throughout

the year. They also need all the support they can get, as honey bee numbers are falling to near catastrophic levels – 30% at the last count – but hopefully the growing public interest in producing honey could help reverse the trend.

If you're interested, sign up for an introductory course run by the British Bee Keeping Association to find out what's involved, or if you don't have room for a hive then you could always adopt one.

www.britishbee.org.uk
www.adoptabeehive.co.uk

Say cheese!

Everyone loves to take photographs. It's now easier than ever to snap a special occasion on your mobile phone and share it within seconds, but what about those everyday scenes that have a fleeting beauty all of their very own?

Like spotting the one balcony in a block of flats that's packed with cheerful hanging baskets and window boxes, or the daisies pushing up through the cracks on the pavement, or the birds tweeting away above the roar of the morning traffic?

Here are some projects to help you capture some of that natural beauty that could be just around the corner:

❋ Why not choose a scene you see every day and take a photo in different weathers.

❋ Or choose a colour and photograph all the natural elements and objects you see in that colour.

❋ Or choose a shape e.g a heart and document all the natural objects that you come across that resemble it to create a gallery or collage.

Try something a bit different and remember there are no rules.

The sky is the limit

How often do you stop and just look up at the sky? According to Gavin Pretor-Pinney, author of *The Cloud Spotters Handbook*, there's a simple antidote to the stresses of modern life that's to be found right above our heads.

"Our lives seem busier than ever" says Gavin, "and everything happens with lightning speed. We have endless emails and alerts to deal with every day, and cloud spotting is a great antidote to that. It's a chance to take a moment out of your day, and slow down to a more relaxed pace. Clouds are fairly formless things, they can take many shapes and encourage you to tap into your creativity, like ink blot drawings, and imagine what they could be."

"You can cloud spot almost anywhere" adds Gavin, "but the ideal location is somewhere wide open with few obstructions, which can equally be out in the countryside or on top of a tall building. I do most of mine in my back garden. I find it's more about your frame of mind than about your location, which makes it a very egalitarian pastime. After all, we all live under the same sky."

What to look for:

Cumulus, Cirrus, Stratus and Cumulonimbus are amongst the most common and easily identified.

❋ Cumulus is a low cloud, puffy like cotton wool and a sign of fair weather. Then there's Cirrus, a high, streaky cloud. It gives a sense of scale to the atmosphere.

❋ Stratus cloud is one we are very familiar with in the UK, it's low lying and grey, and can affect your mood in a negative sense.

❋ Dramatic Cumulonimbus looks like a blacksmith's anvil, rising up to 10 miles high before spreading out. From below it can look very dark and often brings thunder and lightning with it.

Let the kids run wild

I have some fantastic childhood memories of climbing trees, catching tadpoles, making dens and playing hide and seek in the field behind our house. However it seems that these days that you see far fewer kids playing outside, probably due to the greater number of temptations available to keep them indoors (TV, computer games and social networking to name a few).

Parents also seem more wary about letting their kids play outside, and it's a shame that they aren't getting the same opportunities to use their

imaginations in the outdoors and learn how to judge risks for themselves, as well as keeping healthy from all that running around!

Ex teachers Jo Schofield and Fiona Danks, are passionate believers in the benefits of outdoor play and have some great ideas for engaging kids. Here's one from their book, *Make it Wild*, to get the kids started on their next woodland walk (if you can prise them away from the Wii that is…)

Making wonderful woodland puppets

Time and again this activity has proved hugely popular with a range of ages; it is fun, simple and open-ended!

✤ On a walk look out for damp clay in clean ditches or at the edge of a stream or river. Collect a small amount of clay for each person.

✤ Remove any sticks, stones of other debris from the collected clay, and then work it in your hands until it becomes pliable. Roll it into a smooth round ball.

✤ Look for a stick to make your puppet from; it can be a straight stick to make a mariot style puppet, or any shape you like to make a monster or a magical creature. Push the ball of clay firmly onto the stick and mould a head shape.

✤ Look out for loose natural materials to make the features, hair, headdress or whatever you wish. Perhaps you might use seeds, feathers, berries, twigs and leaves – see what you can find.

Bare your sole

What could be nicer than a morning jog along the beach feeling the sand between your toes, or the grass beneath your feet on a woodland trail?

Humans are actually designed to run barefoot. Scientists say that millions of years of evolution have given us strong, large arches that act as a spring when we're running. In parts of Africa, barefoot running has actually been common for years; Ethiopian Olympic gold medalist Abebe Bikila even won his first marathon barefoot in 1960!

So is it safe just to skip out the door sans trainers? It's a good idea to first check with a physiotherapist or at a running shop if you have the correct foot structure to support barefoot running. Someone who pronates or has a flat arch might put strain on their joints if they run without support.

Also, you might want a bit of added protection from hidden nasties on the ground. The slightly neanderthal looking 'Vibram Fivefingers foot glove' has proven enormously popular, reaching sales of $10m in the US, and many sports shoe manufacturers are getting in on the action with their own 'barefoot' trainer designs which look more like an actual trainer but with the flexibility and feel of a foot glove.

Whether you choose to 'glove up' or go fully naked, barefoot running uses different muscles so go slowly to begin with. However, man has been walking barefoot for millions of years so it shouldn't take too long to fall back into step.

Freshen up your 9 to 5

We are now supposed to be living in a golden age of technology where Blackberries, laptops and wireless broadband have made remote working a breeze, and yet we seem as tied to our desks as ever. The traditional 9-5 model of office based working is still going strong, but flexible working can reap huge benefits for both employers and outdoor loving employees.

In his book, *Let my people go surfing*, the founder of outdoor clothing retailer Patagonia, Yvon Chouinard explains how he wanted to redefine what coming to work could be like. "We all had to come to work on the balls of our feet and go up the stairs two steps at a time… We all needed flextime to surf the waves when they were good or ski the powder after a big snowstorm or stay home and take care of a sick child."

Now not all of us are lucky enough to have Yvon Chouinard as our boss, but if you want to reclaim some balance between your work life and outdoor activities, it might be worth making a case for say, working from home one day a week or being employed on freelance basis instead of full time, to allow you more control over your working hours.

Making your case

✿ Research shows that a happy workforce is more productive and more loyal. Flexible working would make you happier, and therefore more motivated and committed.

✿ Consider a 4 day week. If your employer is looking to cut costs, this could be a win-win situation for both of you.

✿ Whatever flexible working plan you go with, suggest a trial run. You can agree goals with your boss that are based on results, not the sheer amount of hours logged, so they can see what you have achieved whilst out of the office.

✿ Be contactable. This will help build trust and might pave the way for a more permanent solution.

Still having trouble convincing the boss? Quote Einstein…

Step away from your desk if you're trying to be creative. Steven Spielberg gets inspired whilst driving, Einstein had his best ideas in the shower, and poets and writers have commonly credited going for a walk with unleashing their creativity.

So next time you're struggling to come up with a killer opening for that important presentation, you've got a rock solid excuse to down tools and head to the park. After all, if it worked for Wordsworth…

Dig for victory

I blame Hugh Fearnley Whittingstall. If it weren't for him and his lush cottage garden being screened into my living room every week, I might never have tried planting my first tomato seed and wouldn't now be in the grip of 'grow your own' fever.

It's an affliction that seems to have affected vast swathes of the British nation, whether it's growing a few runner beans or a whole garden full of brassicas. Waiting lists for allotments in some areas are now preposterously long (up to 40 years in some London boroughs – Source: *Telegraph*), but that doesn't have to hold you back if you fancy trying your hand.

If you haven't got much outside space at home, then patio containers or window boxes are a great way to get started. Salad, chillis, tomatoes, climbing French beans and chard will all live happily in pots and grow bags, and can look just as decorative as flowers.

Whatever container you use, ensure it has drainage holes and add a few broken bits of crockery or old pot in the bottom. Then all you need is some compost, a watering can, and a sunny spot to help your seeds germinate.

 Not only will you soon have a cheap source of fresh vegetables, but growing your own can also help reduce stress, give you a great sense of achievement and helps foster community spirit.

Get an early start

The spring dawn chorus is an incredible crescendo of birdsong that's well worth getting up for, and you can catch it in towns and cities as well as the open countryside.

2nd May is International Dawn Chorus Day, and generally the start of May is considered the best time to hear it. The birds put on a rowdy

show at this time of year to defend their territory and attract a mate, with robins, blackbirds, sky-larks, thrushes and wrens all getting into the mix.

You'll have to set your alarm for around 5am, the hour before dawn, but if that sounds like too much hard work then tune in to www.birdsongradio.com. The original radio station started out as a 20 minute loop tape of birdsong that was being played to fill a spare slot, but it became an unlikely hit, attracting half a million listeners. It was eventually taken off air in 2009 but the website now enables you to listen online or order the CD.

However, nothing beats a live performance, so even if you only ever do it once, set that alarm and brew some coffee, you won't regret it.

Buddy up

"A journey is best measured in friends, not in miles." Tim Cahill

Hate exercising alone, or find it hard to get motivated? Then get an outdoor exercise buddy or two, or five… People who exercise with a friend tend to do it more regularly, help to push each other, and the joint commitment means you're more likely to stick to it. After all, it's one thing to duck out of a session when you've only yourself to answer to, it's quite another to explain it to someone who is already halfway down the road to meet you.

It also turns your exercise session into a sociable occasion, so you get to catch up on their news and stay fit at the same time. So invite work colleagues for a lunch hour jog, or friends for an after work cycle session. If it becomes a regular thing, you could sign up for an event together to have a shared goal to aim for. You'll be printing those customized t shirts in no time, once you can agree on the team name that is…

Experiment with drugs (er, herbal ones of course…)

Next time you have achy muscles after a long run, or need some insect repellent for your camping trip, it might be worth taking a look at what's in the back garden instead of the medicine cabinet.

Ethnobotanist James Wong (how cool is that job title?) studies the relationship between plants and people, and his infectious enthusiasm for the subject landed him his own BBC series, *How to make your own drugs*. He points out that 70% of new medicinal drugs have been developed from natural resources, and we are still as dependant on the natural world as we have ever been.

So give these simple natural remedies a try, as the chances are your usual pills and lotions originated from a plant anyway:

✿ Aloe vera is an easy plant to grow indoors and can be cut and applied directly to burns or any infected or inflamed skin.

✿ Fresh rosemary, cloves, sunflower oil and vodka make a great rub for sore joints and muscles (see his book *Grow Your Own Drugs: A Year With James Wong* for the exact recipe as he also explains the proper techniques for creating balms, creams, tinctures and infusions).

✿ Sage is another good one to grow as it will be happy either in a pot or in the garden, and can be used in a wide range of ailments from sore throats, to swollen joints, to a vitamin packed pick me up if you're feeling tired or down.

Hug a local tree

Trees bring so much to our neighbourhoods. They support wildlife, reduce pollution, and make our streets calmer, more inviting spaces to be in. Certain types of crime could also be reduced by greenery. A study in Chicago showed on two otherwise identical housing estates, the one that had plenty of trees had 30 per cent fewer crimes of violent aggression than one where all the trees had been cut down.

If you're fortunate enough to have council planted trees on your street, then keep an eye out for their welfare especially in the warmer months. In their first few years, trees need a bit of extra loving care during long, dry spells.

If they're starting to look a bit sorry for themselves, you can help by giving them a good soak now and again. Five bucketfuls delivered slowly down their watering pipe should do it (they're all planted with one), and you'll get a great feeling every time you walk past that tree knowing that you've helped it grow.

Go on, give it a hug, we won't tell anyone.

Start your own orchard

Why not plant a fruit tree? It's incredibly satisfying to grow and harvest your own fruit and there's something to suit everyone depending on the space you have available. Try a dwarf apple, cherry or plum in a large pot on your patio, or if you've got a garden then you can go full size.

Fruit trees not only provide delicious pickings for you, but sustain wildlife too and attract pollinating insects which in turn benefit other plants in the area. You'll also be creating a legacy, as the trees you plant will continue to benefit the area and the people living there even if you move away.

You can get plenty of advice on choosing a species that's right for your area and soil conditions, at www.treeforall.org.uk.

Let the train take the strain this weekend

I often wonder, when stuck in traffic on a Friday night with a car full of camping gear, why on earth didn't we take the train? Imagine checking in, tucking in and waking up in the Highlands of Scotland or the Cornish coast.

These days, overnight train travel doesn't mean roughing it either. According to the fantastic train travel advice site www.seat61.com, the "Night Riviera sleeper train is a miniature travelling hotel". On this London to Cornwall service, you can even take your bike for free (but there are only three spaces so be sure to reserve your spot), and dogs are welcome if you want to take Fido for a bracing cliff top walk instead of his usual circuit in the local park.

Alternatively, if you need a fix of glorious glens and lovely lochs, then the Caledonian sleeper allows you to wake up in the Scottish West Highlands, at the foot of Ben Nevis. You can even order haggis and tatties for dinner to get you in the Highland spirit. If you can't bear to head home on the Sunday night, try taking the West Highland line extension onwards to the Isle of Sky, voted *Wanderlust* magazine's best train journey in the world no less. I know where I'd rather be on a Monday morning…

www.firstgreatwestern.co.uk
www.scotrail.co.uk

Become a human Sat Nav

In the age of GPS, we may think we don't need to use traditional forms of natural navigation anymore. But according Tristan Gooley, author of *The Natural Navigator*, it misses the point. "For me it is less about necessity and much more about enjoyment and enrichment."

Gooley taught himself these skills over many years of travel, which have seen him lead expeditions up mountains and across oceans, and he now runs a navigation school in Sussex, teaching groups on the South Downs. He believes that these skills can come in useful in the heart of the city just as much as in the middle of a wilderness, and wants to appeal to those "who enjoy fresh air and have an open mind".

So whether you're heading out to the hills or just round to the corner shop, why not test out Tristan's tips and see if they help to keep you on the right track…

✿ The sun will be due south from the UK when it is highest in the sky, near midday each day.

✿ Tune into what the wind and consequently what the clouds are doing at the start of each day.

✿ All stars move in the night sky, with the important exception of the North Star.

Walk your way around the UK

Apparently only 5% of our New Year resolutions last the entire year. Could it be because these resolutions are too open ended? Professional sportsmen and women often recommend setting yourself a tangible goal, rather than something vague such as "getting fit", and also breaking it down into manageable sections.

Completing one of our national walking trails is a perfect new year goal to set yourself, with varying lengths to choose from like the Beacons Way (100 miles) or the South West Coast path (630 miles). You can arrange your travel and accommodation around whichever section you'll be covering that day or weekend, and you'll get tremendous satisfaction from charting your progress on a map over the course of the year.

If the sheer scale of the goal seems too daunting, then work out mini steps (even 10 minutes of route planning is better than nothing), then visualise yourself achieving it. Most importantly, keep reminding yourself of why you're doing it and reward yourself along the way. In the case of a long distance trail, that's a perfect excuse for plenty of cream tea stops if ever I heard one!

I don't camp darling, I glamp…

Some of us were not made to get muddy. We're perfectly happy to enjoy all that the great outdoors has to offer, as long as it comes with running water and a warm duvet.

Others may have been traumatised by childhood camping experiences, of the kind that Emma Kennedy hilariously tells in her bestselling book, *The tent, The bucket and Me*. "We weren't to know it, but we were in the eye of a force-ten gale" she recalls. "The reason no one was at the campsite was because everyone else knew it was coming. They'd packed up and gone and in the end so did we."

So this is where 'glamping' comes into its own. Think yurts, tipees, shepherd's huts and safari style tents decked out with sheepskin rugs, wood burning stoves and four poster beds. Some might say it's cheating, but technically you're still going back to nature and savouring simple pleasures like lighting a fire and sitting out to watch shooting stars.

The glamping element simply protects you from some of the more unpredictable elements that can make or break a camping trip, such as cold (no problem with a goose down duvet), rain (sounds quite romantic on the roof of an eco pod) and rogue wildlife (have you ever seen a stampeding bull try to open the door of a gypsy caravan?).

Camping is what you make it, whether it's just a tarpaulin in the woods or a Bedouin tent fit for a Saudi prince. The main thing is that you're enjoying the outdoors, with or without a champagne flute.

Check out www.canopyandstars.co.uk and goglamping.net for some great suggestions.

Begin something

"Until one is committed, there is hesitancy, the chance to draw back – Concerning all acts of initiative (and creation), there is one elementary truth that ignorance of which kills countless ideas and splendid plans: that the moment one definitely commits oneself, then Providence moves too… A whole stream of events issues from the decision, raising in one's favor all manner of unforeseen incidents and meetings and material assistance, which no man could have dreamed would have come his way. Whatever you can do, or dream you can do, begin it. Boldness has genius, power, and magic in it. Begin it now." Goethe

"Just do it." Nike

SUMMER

Wild swimming, al fresco feasts, sleeping under the stars... there are so many ways to enjoy the British summer, the only question is how will you fit it all in?

Summer

" Summer afternoon – summer afternoon; to me those have always been the two most beautiful words in the English language."
Henry James

Find your urban oasis

There's a secret little spot, about five minutes walk from my office, where I go to escape from the hustle and bustle. It's not big, a hundred square metres at most, but it's green, lush and full of hidden corners perfect for chilling out during a stressful working day. It's surrounded on all sides by office blocks, but the garden is full of trees, flowers, ponds and the sound of birdsong instead of the hum of traffic.

These parks, commons, gardens and squares act as lungs for our cities, as well as a focal point for local communities, helping to reduce stress, boost health and can even cut crime. London alone is made up of 38% green space.

However, despite all these benefits our precious green spaces are constantly under threat from development or noise pollution. So if you love your local park or community garden then you need to use it, support it, and if it is under threat then shout about it. People of Britain, your green spaces need YOU.

Find your nearest green space:

www.green-space.org.uk
farmgarden.org.uk
www.capitalgrowth.org

Preen your pavement

Do you pass somewhere every day that looks unloved? Maybe a scrubby border or a bare roundabout that needs some cheering up? Even if you don't have a garden of your own, you can make any neglected patch of land near your home a bit more beautiful as well as a haven for birds and wildlife, with a spot of 'guerilla gardening'..

What's it all about then?

Former advertising executive, Richard Reynolds's gardening crusade began on his housing estate in Elephant and Castle in 2004. Noticing that the council wasn't paying much attention to the communal flower beds, he decided to take matters into his own hands, sneaking out at 2am for some undercover mulching and planting.

Soon Reynolds found himself tapping in to an international movement of activist gardeners – from Montreal to Brisbane – who take on unused public land and transform it into lush, cultivated flower displays and allotments.

Technically, it is illegal to plant on property that does not belong to you. Despite this, there are now guerrilla gardening cells all over the world that carry out this beautification work, which they believe improves neighbourhoods and encourages regeneration in run down and neglected areas.

So if you fancy do your own bit of 'illicit cultivation', then have a go at making your very own 'seed bomb':

❋ First identify your target area, whether it's some disused land or a grass verge.

❋ Then bind your seeds together preferably with some biodegradable material such as clay, or if you can't find any then try using a balloon like a water bomb.

❋ Add some soil and water so that the seeds can germinate when they land, and then launch away!

www.guerrillagardening.org

Wax lyrical

*"I will arise and go now, and go to Innisfree,
And a small cabin build there, of clay and
   wattle made;
Nine bean rows will I have there, a hive for
   the honeybee,
And live alone in the bee-loud glade."*

From 'The Lake Isle of Innisfree' by
William Butler Yeats

Ever watched a sunset or reached a mountain summit and felt inspired to put pen to paper? When you're back in the city, stuck in the office or on a crowded train, a poem can be a powerful way of transporting yourself back to that place and time, helping you to escape your daily stresses.

Be prepared

First, take a pen and paper with you on your outdoor jaunts. That way you'll always be prepared should inspiration strike.

Make full use of your senses.

Don't just look around you, but also close your eyes and listen to the sounds of nature. Listen to the wind, the birds, the bugs, the grass growing... anything.

Lastly, take a deep breath in and sense your surroundings. Can you smell the trees? The sea?

Just write

Think of some key words that come to mind when you observe your surroundings and write them down. When you start writing, don't edit or go back. This way, your immediate feelings will be more easily captured in your work.

Finishing touches

Take a quick look over your poem and make small adjustments until you are satisfied with the result. There are various poetry styles and techniques you could try, like haikus or rhyming poems, but the important thing is to make a start without worrying about the form too much.

Now you can just slip it in your pocket, ready for those moments when you need to escape to broader horizons, even if it's only in your mind…

Have a fresh air feast

One of the most memorable picnics I ever had involved a beach, a storm, and some cold sausages. An unexpected weather front had moved in off the sea, but rather than run off the beach with all the other tourists, we huddled under a parasol, wrapped the picnic blanket round our legs and watched the black clouds approach.

Sure enough it poured down for a while, but some chilled prosecco soon took the edge off and we were rewarded with one of the most

spectacular rainbows I have ever seen. Only a handful of surfers and us were left to enjoy it, which made it even more special.

This I believe is the secret to British picnicking. If you wait for the perfect weather, then you'll be waiting all summer. But if you have a picnic kit waiting in the car or by the door for whenever the mood strikes, and are prepared to stick it out come rain or shine, then you'll be guaranteed some fantastic memories.

What to pack?

✿ Have a decent cool bag and some ice packs already in the freezer which can be popped in at a moment's notice.

✿ Packing proper crockery and cutlery allows you to concentrate on enjoying the food, rather than trying to figure out how to balance a pork pie on your knee.

✿ Other essentials are a corkscrew for unforeseen celebrations and toasts, and a couple of tea lights in jam jars to create an instant romantic atmosphere.

✿ A simple groundsheet (available from any outdoor or camping shop) is fantastically versatile, either as extra ground cover or can be slung up as a tarp with some bungee cords to provide you with an instant 'roof'.

What to eat?

All food just seems to taste better outdoors but be imaginative with your picnic. Local ingredients can add something special, whether its eggs from the local farmer, veg from the honesty box in the village you passed through, or even some freshly caught fish (possibly caught by your own fair hand?).

Whatever your feast consists of, eating outdoors is one of those summer pleasures that is all the sweeter for being fleeting. A memory to sustain you on a wind lashed January day…

Tune into the weather

They might not beat the MET office app on your iPhone, but recognising these age old signs for forecasting weather could come in handy next time you're out and about, and they'll definitely impress your friends.

❋ Early morning mists and dew in summer mean a warm dry day, whereas rising air means rain, so no dew in the morning

❋ A pine cone closes up in moist weather to protect its seeds

❋ Easterly winds bring dry weather, hot in summer and cold in winter.

❋ Crickets churp when the sun is out

❋ Swallows fly high in good weather as their food supply (insects) is carried high on thermal currents.

Take the plunge

Everyone seems to be at it. Wild swimming is in the papers, it's on TV, and yet there is still some confusion over what the term actually means. Is it the same as open water swimming? Do outdoor swimming pools count? Do you have to do it naked?

The popularity of wild swimming has increased hugely in recent years, fuelled by the desire to get back to Nature and the publication of guides like *Wild Swim* by Kate Rew, founder of the Outdoor Swimming Society. NASA have even studied it and found that our bodies adapt after repeated cold water immersion, bringing down blood pressure and cholesterol, toning muscle and increasing libido!

Despite this abundance of information however, many of us aren't too sure where and when we can do it safely and enjoyably. One of the best places to start is the OSS website. Here you'll find tips on safety, improving your technique and a swim map to help you find the nearest wild swimming spot. That said, never wild swim alone. You can find organized swims or arrange meet ups with people in your area, via the society's facebook page.

Converts say they love the sense of freedom, and of closeness to nature. "You do become a bit evangelical – it puts you back in touch with yourself" says Kate Rew.

For the record, wild swimming is basically the same thing as open water swimming, outdoor pools don't really count but are a good place to start, and no you don't have to swim naked (unless of course you want to, it has been known..)

www.outdoorswimmingsociety.com

Take the lead

Whether it's taking charge of the map when out walking with friends, or showing your nephew or niece how to stand up on a surfboard, these valuable leadership skills could have a knock on affect on your work too.

Sharing your knowledge and experience, welcoming newcomers and reasoning with a group to come up with a fair decision, are all skills that can be beneficial for your career as well as being personally rewarding.

The Ramblers Society run workshops for wannabe walk leaders, covering everything from how to select a suitable walk to safety, first aid, rights of way and the law, navigation skills and diplomacy skills (crucial when choosing which pub to stop at!)

There are also plenty of short coaching courses around for different outdoor sports. Your local club may even subsidise the fees if you agree to assist with coaching new members on a regular basis. Check with the head organisation for your favourite activity (BCU for kayakers, BMC for mountaineers etc).

So don't be afraid to step up and take charge, it could be the start of a whole new career.

www.ramblers.org.uk

Just when you thought it was safe to go back in the water…

 If you spot a fin in the water this summer, don't go run screaming for the nearest lifeguard. It's far more likely to be a dolphin, porpoise, basking shark or even the back end of a seal, all of whom are native to British waters.

The Marine Conservation Society needs an army of volunteer wildlife spotters to help them create a snapshot of the distribution of dolphins, whales and porpoises around the coast. In turn this feeds into scientific discussions on abundance and distribution. They also want to hear from you if you spot any rarer visitors to our waters such as leather back turtles and jellyfish.

So next time you're near the coast, why not park yourself up with a picnic and a pair of binoculars, and spend an hour or two scanning the shore. You might be amazed by what breaks the surface…

www.mcsuk.org

Get fit with Fido

 If motivation is your main bugbear when it comes to heading outdoors, then a canine companion might actually be the best personal trainer you could wish for. Apparently dog walkers get on average seven hours exercise a week, whilst rest of us only manage around 1hr 20mins.

You'll be burning up to 240 calories an hour, and as a pet owner you'll also be benefitting from lower cholesterol, lower blood pressure, lower stress levels and a stronger immune system.

If you don't have a dog, volunteer to walk a rescue dog for the RSPCA or help out an elderly or house bound dog owner via the Cinammon Trust. Just go easy on the doggie treats, or else Fido's waistline might start expanding just as yours is shrinking!

Set up camp in the garden

 Camping is one of summer's great pleasures, but there is always a certain amount of preparation and planning involved. Finding the time to get away, packing up the car and having to observe strict campsite rules can be enough to put anyone off.

So what if you had to look no further than your own back garden? Where there are no rules, pets are always allowed, there are unlimited refreshments, and you can bring as many luxuries as you want (candlesticks anyone?).

So pitch the tent and light that campfire (usual safety rules apply of course, unless you want a nicely scorched lawn). The neighbours might wonder what on earth you're up, but invite them over for a campfire sing along and they'll soon be won round.

Or if the night temperatures are balmy then why not drag a mattress outside and sleep under the stars? Just remember that your dawn wake up call might be earlier than usual, but what nicer way to be woken than with bird song and soft pink skies. Certainly beats the usual bleeping alarm.

Be picky

Pick Your Own farms were plentiful in East Sussex where I grew up. I have many happy, hazy memories of summer afternoons spent between rows of strawberry plants. My preferred picking technique at the time was to 'taste test' the fruit before putting it in the basket. Let's just say my baskets never came back very full…

In my humble opinion, fruit and vegetables from PYO farms have unbeatable flavour and can be tremendous value for money (expect to pay around half what you'd pay in many supermarkets). They're also better for the environment, as PYO means minimum packaging and zero food miles (apart from those you clock up when taking your harvest home).

There are plenty of PYO's within easy reach of most major towns and cities, just type your postcode into *www.pickyourown.info*.

Here's a really simple strawberry jam recipe that I used to make with my mum, to use up any surplus pickings (not that there were often any!):

Ingredients

500g crushed fresh hulled strawberries
700g caster sugar
1 (13g) sachet of pectin
180ml water

❋ Mix the crushed strawberries with sugar, and leave to stand for 10 minutes.

❋ Meanwhile, stir the pectin into the water in a small saucepan. Bring to the boil over medium-high heat, and boil for 1 minute. Stir the boiling water into the strawberries.

❋ Allow to stand for 3 minutes before pouring into jars or other storage containers.

❋ Place tops on the containers, and leave for 24 hours. Place in the freezer, and store frozen until ready to use. Yum.

Create a mini wildlife sanctuary

You might not always associate urban areas with wildlife, but there is plenty going on if you look a little more closely. Where I work in central London, there is a community garden which claims to be home to the West End's only toad population!

In fact according to the London Wildlife Trust, the capital is home to some surprising species, including Peregrine falcons, water voles, bats and some unique 'city' plants which thrive in the warmer urban environment such as Tower mustard and London rocket.

Wherever you live, it's vital that we create city homes for wildlife. Many creatures that are declining in the countryside, such as the common frog, song thrush and hedgehog can thrive in domestic gardens and other areas if we provide the right conditions for them. Here are some ideas:

❁ Plant flowers to provide pollen and nectar for bees, butterflies and other insects all year round such as buddleia, lavender and thyme.

❁ Create a pond or just use an upturned bin lid or a sunken washing bowl filled with water. Make sure it has one sloping side to allow creatures an easy way out, and add lots of plants.

❁ Let a patch of your lawn grow longer, as this encourages wild flowers, provides shelter for small mammals and food for some butterfly caterpillars.

❁ Garden in a sustainable way, by using fewer chemicals and avoiding peat. -Choose wood from sustainable sources, recycle all you can and save water.

The results might not be instant, but with a bit of TLC, your garden, patio or balcony could become a mini sanctuary for all sorts of city loving wildlife.

A home from home... by the sea

The popularity of beach huts has soared in recent years, and it's easy to see why. Full of colour and character, these little refuges allow you to spend time by the sea in relative comfort no matter what the capricious British summer weather throws at you.

Despite offering few home comforts (no hot water, toilets or sleeping areas), beach huts attract a devoted following, with many families passing them on through the generations and using them through summer and winter.

If you want to try hut life for yourself, you can rent them by the day, the week, or buy one outright though be warned, the waiting lists in popular spots can be pretty lengthy. Also, prices have been known to soar to in excess of £100,000, but for some it's worth the cost for a little bit of paradise by the sea.

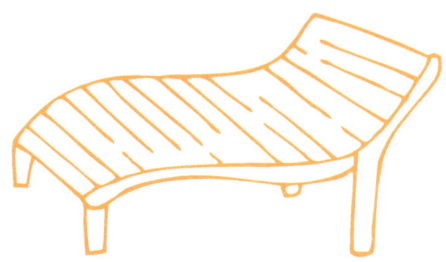

Popular beach hut spots:
❁ Mudeford, Dorset
❁ Scarborough, North Yorkshire
❁ Walton on the Naze, Essex
❁ Whitstable, Kent

Rent and buy:
www.beach-huts.com

Get on the bat trail

Whether you're a fan of bats or not, there are 17 species in the UK and they are being forced to move closer to towns and cities because their traditional roosting sites in the countryside are being destroyed and food sources killed off by pesticides.

Your most likely to spot them at dusk when they're out feeding on insects (not fair skinned maidens!), but don't worry they're totally harmless. In fact, they're so small they could fit through a hole the diameter of your index finger. Take an evening stroll near trees, water, or street lights because their food is attracted to the light.

You might also see them in your roof or the crevices of buildings, but don't disturb them as they're actually protected by law. Or you could try and attract them by planting night scented flowers, or installing a 'bat box' in the garden.

If you prefer to keep them at arms length but still want to experience the thrill of a night time bat walk, The Wildlife Trust and various nature reserves and wetland centres organise special walks, which teach you about the different species and the 'clicks' they make. A few hooting owls and darkening Skies should add to the atmosphere, mwahahahaha…..

www.bats.org.uk

We can work it out

 Learning a new outdoor sport can be a bit like dating. At first you can't get enough, it's like an addiction. There's a lot to learn, perhaps a few disagreements but you quickly make up and go back for more.

However as time passes, its starts to feel less exciting. You're over the learning curve and things have gone a bit stale. Is it time to move on?

When my relationship with running hit the doldrums, I realised it was time to spice things up a bit. We'd had lots of good times, and maybe the problem wasn't the running, it was actually me?

I signed up for a charity 10k, introduced some sprinting and hills to make the workouts more challenging, and took up pilates to introduce something totally new. As it turned out, pilates complimented my running beautifully as it helps to lengthen muscles and assist recovery. Within a few months I had fallen back in love with running all over again.

So the lesson here? Don't walk away from your first outdoor love, work on your relationship, and you might just find that the two of you can enjoy a second honeymoon...

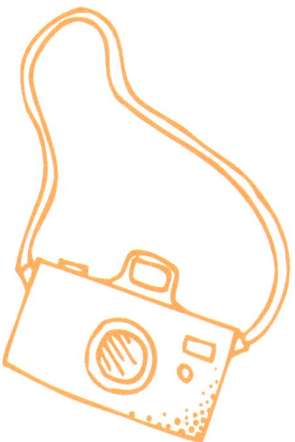

Head for the open road

 Campervans represent total freedom. In a camper, you are master of your own destiny. No need to adhere to strict train or bus timetables, you can just hit the road whenever you feel like it.

There's no need to spend hours packing the car either as a camper is self contained, plus it keeps you warm and dry no matter what the British weather throws at you. Best of all, they have a proper two ringed stove so you can indulge in gourmet meals. Who says camping food has to be basic?

Make the neighbours jealous with the smell of this one-pan breakfast frittata recipe wafting out of the cabin:

Ingredients:

1 pepper
3 rashers bacon
6 eggs
2 tbsp chives
2 tbsp parmesan

❋ Heat some oil in a pan, then soften the peppers for 5 mins, followed by the bacon for another 5 mins.

❋ Beat the eggs with some chives, parmesan and seasoning in a separate dish. When the peppers are soft, add the egg mixture and leave to cook for 5 mins, or until the bottom is golden.

❋ Then put the pan under a grill for another 5 mins until the top is set.

❋ Cut into wedges and tuck in!

If you want more campervan friendly recipes, get hold of Martin Dorey's *Camper Van Cookbook*, a treasure trove of delicious recipes and tips for making the most of camper van living. Make this the summer of the camper.

www.campervanlife.com

AUTUMN

*Kick up the leaves, forage in the hedgerows
and roam the hills and paths without the summer crowds.
Autumn is the time to reclaim the outdoors
and savour the shortening days.*

Autumn

" No spring nor summer beauty hath such grace,
As I have seen in one autumnal face."
John Donne

Come on baby, light my fire

If you're out in the garden at this time of year, or even brave enough for a spot of camping, then it will always be more cheerful with a roaring campfire to warm your cockles. However, not all of us have Ray Mears style survival knowledge, but this lighting method should be simple enough for anyone to try:

❂ Collect your wood. You'll need three types, kindling, sticks and larger pieces. Make sure they're naturally fallen from the tree, and dry.

❂ Choose your site. If you're in the countryside, choose a designated spot or one where there is evidence of a previous campfire. If not, then make sure it's sheltered from the wind, far enough away from your tent or anything flammable, and won't kill any nearby plants. Dig a fire pit and ring it with stones.

❂ Build the campfire. Place your kindling in a pyramid shape, with the larger pieces on the outside. If you need a helping hand, by all means stick a firelighter or two in there, but never lighter fluid. Then light your materials, and once the flame is going, then you can gradually add your sticks and larger bits of wood.

Et voila, a cosy campfire to take the edge off a chilly day. Now where did I put those marshmallows?

Dare yourself

"Man cannot discover new oceans unless he has the courage to lose sight of the shore."
Andre Gide

Feel some national pride

Believe it or not, back in 1932 much of Britain was actually out of bounds. However, some plucky ramblers decided to change all that with a mass trespass up Kinder Scout, and eventually managed to get the National Parks and Access to the Countryside Act passed in 1949. Two years later, the Peak District, Britain's first National Park, was created.

Today about 10 per cent of Britain's land area is protected within the fifteen National Parks, so there's bound to be one near you. The nearest to London are the Norfolk Broads, the New Forest and the newly created South Downs, whilst Northerners are spoilt for choice with the Yorkshire Dales, the Lake District and Northumberland National Park.

Wales also has gorgeous variety in the shape of rugged mountains (Snowdonia) and a wave lashed coastline (Pembrokeshire), and the Scottish Highlands probably crowns them all in terms of awe inspiring peaks, valleys, and wildlife.

However, our National Parks are suffering. Steep funding cuts were announced in 2010, and the parks are increasingly relying on volunteers and donations. More than ever, we need to help our parks by boosting visitor numbers, reinvesting in the local economy and making sure we don't leave a trace. So what more excuse do you need for organising that weekend away, and showing some love for our national parks?

www.nationalparks.gov.uk

Create an outdoor office

Who wouldn't want to work at the bottom of the garden? Birdsong instead of the hum of the photocopier and a view of your flowerbeds instead of the office block opposite, what's not to love? Welcome to the wonderful world of shed working.

Whether you are a home worker, or have a flexible working arrangement with your employer, you'll be joining a long tradition of creative thinkers who have used garden offices (think Roald Dahl, Henry Moore, Peter Gabriel, Grieg…)

Alex Johnson, founder of www.shedworking.co.uk and author of Shedworking: The alternative workplace revolution, gives his tips for creating the ultimate outdoor work space:

❋ Unless your existing shed is very sturdy, your best bet may be to knock it down and build something new.

❋ You'll need to consider two key practical issues, insulation and security.

❋ You should also think about insurance if you'll have work visitors to the garden office, and of course planning permission if you intend to run any kind of unusual business from it or make large scale structural alterations.

❋ If you're quite handy, then definitely have a go at constructing your own. We've profiled lots of people on Shedworking who have built their own garden office very successfully and there's an entire chapter in the book devoted to examples of people who have either used kits or built it entirely from their own designs.

Grow you own bouquet

What could bring the outdoors in more powerfully than a bunch of freshly cut flowers? The scent of fresh flowers actually increases feelings of compassion and kindness, reduces anxiety and helps you feel more energetic and enthusiastic. Powerful stuff.

A staggering 90% of our flowers are now imported from as far away as Africa or South America, but a small number of British growers such as www.wigglywigglers.co.uk are championing our home grown flowers again. Locally grown flowers also stay fresh for longer because they' don't have to be refrigerated, and you're more likely to find unusual or delicate native varieties since local growers don't have to worry about transporting them.

DIY it

The ultimate of course is to create your own cutting garden. These were invented by 19th-century head gardeners who grew cut flowers with the same principles they applied to vegetable growing. Be sure to prepare the ground well, plan something for every season and make sure there are enough to ensure a good crop. Here are some of my favourites, great for colour, fragrance and easy to look after:

❋ California poppies (brief but unforgettable)

❋ Sweet peas (smell gorgeous and will keep flowering as long as you keep picking)

❋ Nasturtiums (double up as an edible salad!)

❋ Sunflowers (all they need is sunshine and love, these babies will shoot up and are guaranteed to cheer up the garden whether you pick them or leave them in situ).

Tune in and chill out

Ever felt the need to plug in and zone out from honking cars and screaming sirens? Most of us spend our days surrounded by the stress-inducing sounds of vehicles, TVs and the hum of electronic equipment. But listening to ambient nature sounds could hold the key to reducing stress and provide a more relaxing atmosphere.

The sound of steady, rhythmic ocean waves has been proven to provide a sense of relaxation and calm, and singing birds are associated with feelings of joyfulness. Storm sounds can also help you to relax or concentrate on work, whilst more consistent sounds, like rain or waterfalls, are supposed to act like a white noise machine that masks household noises such as fridges, heaters and creaking floors, and could help light sleepers and babies sleep better.

So what if you don't happen to live by the sea or live round the corner from a rainforest? Nature sounds CDs and albums are often available in

New Age shops or on *amazon.co.uk* (do a search for the *'Ambient Heaven' range*).

Alternatively, use a small voice recorder or voice memo app on your iPhone to record some natural sounds next time you're outdoors. Then you can be transported away from the rush hour stress at the touch of a button…

Help Britain's beaches

Did you know that for every footstep you take on a beach, there are two pieces of litter? Sadly, marine wildlife get entangled in the litter and can accidentally ingest it, often leading to death from starvation. Ninety per cent of fulmars found dead around the North Sea have plastic in their stomachs.

What can I do to help?

Every year on the third weekend of September, the Marine Conservation Society (MCS) organises a beach litter survey which is then used as a snapshot of the state of marine and beach litter around the UK.

More than 300 UK beaches take part in the survey, know as The Big Beachwatch so there is bound to be one near you. The MCS's Scottish projects officer Anne Saunders, says "We need the public's help to clean and survey our beaches to help tackle the relentless tide of litter threatening our beaches and wildlife".

So sign up, grab a pair of wellies and some bin bags, and help our beaches become plastic free.

Lights, camera and action!

If the video clips from your weekend adventures are anything like mine, they'll usually consist of wobbly shots of pretty landscapes, and any sound obliterated by howling wind.

However, affordable digital video cameras and easy-to-use editing software now mean there's no excuse for not turning out something worthy of a YouTube viral. It just takes a bit of forward thinking. Here are some tips for discovering your inner Spielberg:

❁ Have an idea of what story do you want to tell. Are you planning to reach the summit of a particular peak? Looking for a particular country pub on your bike ride? Bear in mind how to show this in the shots you choose.

❁ Wherever possible, use a tripod. It makes a huge difference.

❁ Bad audio is guaranteed to have people switching off. If you don't have wireless mics (which includes most of us!) then avoid recording any dialogue in the wind. Seek out somewhere sheltered and away from background noise if possible.

❁ Wildlife. A good zoom lens can come in handy here, and don't get too close to large animals. They may not appreciate a camera in their face when they're busy munching grass.

❁ Using music always adds plenty of drama to a video, but make sure you're only screening it at home. If it goes on the internet and you haven't got permission from the record label to use the music, you could end up paying some pretty expensive rights fees.

❁ Don't be restricted to just what's moving across the screen. Use camera tricks—tilts, pans, and zooms—to capture the action and convey the drama of the moment.

❁ Finally, upload your finished masterpiece to the FAF facebook page, and share your adventures with our online community!

Do nothing

Yes you heard right. I said nothing. Zilch. Rien. It might not come naturally, or be something you've done since you were a child, but slowing right down can bring unexpected rewards.

Find a quiet spot, preferably in your garden, a local park, a field or on the beach. Somewhere you can take in the sky, feel the breeze, listen to the birds and just watch. Eventually, possibly, the wildlife will start to ignore your presence and carry on its business.

Watch, listen, melt into the background, and let nature come to you…

Lend a helping hand

 We've all heard a million times how rewarding volunteering can be, but it's also hard to find time for one more thing when your schedule is already packed. However, what if you were able to combine learning new skills with getting fit and contributing to a community project all at the same time? Surely that's time well spent.

The key is to find a successful volunteering placement to matches your outdoor interests, and you'll be much more motivated and probably already have some existing knowledge to share.

Where to start?

The Green Gym, run by BTCV offers opportunities to take part in various practical projects, from clearing woodland to rebuilding footpaths. You meet new people, burn some serious calories and look out over gorgeous countryside for a few hours instead the four walls on a gym.

Or if growing your own is more your thing, then sign up to help out with *Thrive*. This charity help to rehabilitate people with disabilities through gardening, and operates a box scheme to bring plants to disabled people who want to garden but can't leave their homes.

The government campaign website, www.muckin4life.direct.gov.uk also has a fantastic database of conservation-oriented volunteering opportunities across the country.

Have a snack attack

Forget endorphin highs, amazing views or a great sense of achievement. Often the only thing that really persuades me to finish a long run/climb a mountain/jump into a freezing cold lake, is the promise of a fat slab of cake afterwards. Or a chunky flapjack. Or a rocky road-bar oozing with gooey marsh-mallows… well, you get the idea.

Whether you just see food as fuel, or the reward for all your hard work, it's crucial to keep your energy levels up with the right slow burning ingredients.

This yummy flapjack recipe has rescued me on many a long walk with a nice slow release of energy. Tailor it to your own weird and wonderful tastes (marmite and banana - is that just me?) and you can also adjust how much butter and sugar they contain if you're being extra virtuous:

Nice (and just a bit naughty) flapjacks

225g rolled oats
55g raisins
25g almonds
55g soft apricots
25g dried sliced bananas
115g light brown sugar
55g golden syrup
170ml sunflower oil

✤ Preheat the oven to 180C/350F/Gas Mark 4.

✤ Mix the oats and the raisins. Cut the almonds, apricots and bananas into   small chunks and mix

✤ Put the sugar into a medium-sized saucepan, adding the syrup and then the oil. Set over a low heat and stir until the sugar has dissolved. Take care not to let the oil get too hot, it just needs to be warm, then stir in the oat mixture and tip into a 30cm x 20cm non stick baking tray. Spread evenly and pat firmly into the tray.

✤ Bake for 15 minutes or until pale gold. Remove from the oven and as it begins to cool, cut into 12 bars. Leave to cool completely, remove from the tray and place on kitchen paper to soak up excess oil before wrapping individually and storing chilled.

While shepherds watch their flocks by night...

You might not expect to see a flock of sheep grazing on local parkland, but they are becoming an increasingly common sight in our towns and cities as councils choose to use them as a cheaper and greener alternative to noisy and polluting lawnmowers.

People are also queuing up to become volunteer shepherds, with Brighton Council having to put applicants on a waiting list due to overwhelming demand. Fans of shepherding say that the animals are very calming to be around, and clambering up and down hillsides as well as pulling sheep out of hedges will keep you fit.

If you fancy a bit of urban shepherding, then contact your local Council to find out if there is a scheme running near you, or if you want to keep a flock of your own then an alternative is to rent land away from home. *The Small Shepherds Club* can help, and has seen a 50% increase in their membership since 2002 so there will be plenty of other shepherds to give you advice on this baaa-vellous hobby... (sorry, couldn't resist).

Forage your own supper

The popularity of wild food foraging has grown massively in recent years, and it's easy to see why. What could be more fun than heading out the back door with a basket and a guide book, to source your own supper? It also requires you to slow down, pause and look, and be much more aware of your natural surroundings.

Of course a major aspect of foraging is also knowing what to avoid, especially in the mushroom department. There are plenty of great courses and books available (Richard Mabey's *Food for Free* is considered a classic), but local knowledge is always best.

Here are some choice morsels to look out for depending on the season, and a super easy elderflower cordial recipe. Bon appétit!

Spring/early summer – elderflower, nettles, samphire, wild garlic

Autumn – hazelnuts, rosehips, sloes, mushrooms, elderberries

Elderflower Cordial

Ingredients

30 elderflower heads
1.7litres/3 pints boiling water
900g/2lb caster sugar
50g/2oz citric acid (available from chemists)

❂ Gently rinse over the elderflowers to remove any dirt or little creatures.

❂ Pour the boiling water over the sugar in a very large mixing bowl. Stir well and leave to cool.

❂ Add the citric acid and then the flowers.

❂ Leave in a cool place for 24 hours, stirring occasionally.

❂ Strain through some muslin and transfer to sterilised bottles.

Go clubbing

Joining a local club can be one the most effective and sociable ways to learn any new activity. It helps keep you motivated, and you'll benefit from the experience of other members meaning you'll learn faster. Being a member also allows you to borrow or hire club equipment without the responsibility of storing it or insuring it, and usually at a pretty good discount too.

I learnt to kayak following a chance encounter with the local kayaking club during a lazy afternoon stroll along the towpath. Before I knew it they had me signed up for a free taster session, which soon turned into a weekly ritual of river trips with outdoorsy locals who went on become firm friends (quite an achievement in a city where strangers barely make eye contact!).

Contact the main organisation for your chosen activity for a list of certified clubs, or check out *www.meetup.com* for more informal groups. If there's nothing in your immediate area, you could even start up your own via www.meetup.com or create a facebook group.

Monkey around

Remember clambering up trees when you were a kid? Thought those days were over? Well a growing number of professional tree climbing companies don't think so.

Paul McCathie from *Goodleaf Tree Climbing* based on the Isle of Wight explains why messing about in the tree tops can bring out the big kid in everybody. "Our tree climbing is about your own personal achievement, there's no pressure to reach the top. It's always good to push yourself, but our climbing is all about having fun – it's not a military exercise!"

Paul teaches a special technique for tree climbing that uses leg muscles as opposed to upper body muscles, as well as rope and harness just to be on the safe side. So, if you are reasonably fit and have the right mental attitude, then in theory you can climb trees. "The rope and harness enable to you to get to places in the tree you wouldn't normally be able to" he says, "plus it's brilliant to be able to swing around when you're 40 ft in the air!"

I can't make it to Isle of Wight, but there's a tasty looking tree at the bottom of my garden…

"It's always best to talk to a professional arborist before attempting any sort of personal tree climbing" Paul advises. "Other than that, a high sturdy tree with wide, open branches is what we look for. An old English Oak is just about perfect."

Or try a *Go Ape* tree rope course. There are 27 across the country, so there's bound to be one near you.

www.goodleaf.co.uk
www.goape.co.uk

Have a larder on your window sill

A pot or window box of herbs is a really simple way to bring the outside in, especially if you don't have any outdoor space or live in a block of flats.

There's nothing quite like the aroma of freshly picked herbs wafting through the house as you prepare dinner, and some of the easiest to grow are mint, bay, rosemary and oregano which can go with lots of dishes and drinks.

First, find a suitable container. You can be as creative as you like as long as you add some drainage holes in the bottom, or use a simple plastic pot but place it inside something more attractive. Then fill the pot with soil based compost, sow your seeds according to the back of the packet and keep well watered on a light windowsill. Easy peasy, lemon squeezy!

My herby must haves:

❋ For the sunny side of the house I grow basil, chives, oregano, lemon thyme and you could also add a creeping rosemary to drape over the edge.

❋ On the shady side of the house, I find it easier to sow a salad herb window box which has been known to include a variety of wild rocket, chervil, French parsley or red mustard.

My favourite mint Mojito recipe

2 oz light rum
10 mint leaves (freshly picked.)
1-2 tablespoons sugar
1/2 lime, cut into 4 wedges
Club soda

❋ Put mint, lime wedges, and rum in a long glass. Use wooden spoon, lightly crush the ingredients until the aroma of the mint is released.

❋ Add the sugar, ice, and club soda and stir until the mint is spread evenly throughout your drink and the sugar is dissolved. Enjoy!

Mess about in boats

Britain offers over 2000 miles of waterways for us to canoe and kayak at our leisure, some of them running through our towns and cities.

However, it's not quite as simple as slipping your boat into the water and setting off. Current access rights do make things a bit confusing as only 2% of rivers in England and Wales have public access, with most river access being privately owned.

So how can I get on the water?

Look for a local canoe club who can train you up with the required skills as well as organising guided trips to build up experience. When you're ready to venture out under your own steam (though it's strongly advised that you never canoe or kayak alone), then contact The British Canoe Union which has an Access Officer in each region, and can advise you about accessing local waters.

If you want to make a weekend of it, there are plenty of adventure companies to choose from but one of our favourites is www.thecanoeman.com, run by former pensions advisor turned outdoor man, Mark Wilkinson. His one day and weekend trails through the Norfolk Broads can be guided, self guided, or even include bush craft lessons if you really want to get back to nature!

Be a rock star for a day

Always wanted to hear crowds of people screaming your name? Then sign up for a charity race. There's nothing like coming down the home straight, exhausted but spurred on by complete strangers calling out personal encouragement. That is exactly what got me through the last stage of a 10k Cancer Research race, on a hot September day when my throat was parched and even the promise of a giant slice of cake at the end wasn't enough to keep me going!

Signing up to a charity race is also a sure fire way to guarantee that you finish what you started. Once you've signed up, set up your sponsorship page, and told all your friends, there's no going back. The charity is counting on you, your sponsors are counting on you, and you just know it's going to feel amazing when you finally cross that finish line. So go on, don't think about it, do it before you change your mind.

Some classic UK endurance events to tick off the "do before you die" list:

* London Marathon
* BUPA Great North Run
* London to Brighton bike ride
* Three Peak Challenge

One for the girls

Why blow the budget on expensive cosmetics, when some of the best and cheapest ingredients might be available in your garden or local grocers? You can't get much closer to nature than having it spread across your t zone! Give these dead easy treatments a go:

Strawberry face mask (great for oily skins)

Mash up three strawberries, apply, sit back for 10mins then rinse. See, told you it was easy!

Avocado mask (great for dry skins).

Same as above except with half a mashed avocado

Herbal foot reviver

Soak your feet in a bucket of warm water with some added sprigs of rosemary, lavender and sea salt.

Super shine your hair

After shampooing, give your hair a final rinse your hair with four cups of water with an added cup of either lemon juice (for blondes) or crushed rosemary (for brunettes).

Slow down

"Adopt the pace of nature: her secret is patience."
Ralph Waldo Emerson

WINTER

Whether you choose to venture out on a crisp and frosty morning, or snuggle up with a good adventure story, there's lots to love about the outdoors in winter.

Winter

"There's no such thing as bad weather, only the wrong clothes".
Billy Connolly

Be a bookworm

Some days it really is too bleak to go outside. The rain is lashing, the wind is howling and your socks are frozen solid on the washing line.

These are the days that a good, old fashioned adventure story is just what's required. Preferably one that makes the hairs on your neck stand up, your heart beat faster, and leaves you wanting to pack your bags and hop on the next plane to somewhere unpronounceable.

No one story is the same. Some are deeply moving, of triumph against all the odds (Joe Simpson's *Touching the Void*), whilst others remind you how powerful and unforgiving Nature can really be (Sebastian Junger's *The Perfect Storm*). Here are some of my all time favourites to get you started...

* Ellen MacArthur *Taking on the world*
* Ben Fogle and James Cracknell *The Crossing*
* Sir Edmund Hilary *The view from the summit*
* Pete Goss *Close to the wind*

Fatten up the birds

The birds in your garden might struggle a bit over the winter as their usual food supplies start to dwindle, so why not give them a helping hand with this tasty (for them!) bird cake recipe:

* First of all, find a container. An empty coconut shell, plastic cup or yoghurt pot works well. Make a hole in the bottom of your container, poke the string through, then tie a twig to the bottom to make a perch.

* Then make your bird cake. Birds need protein and fat, so make them their favourite snack by pouring melted fat (suet or lard) onto a mixture of ingredients like seeds, nuts, dried fruit, oatmeal, cheese and cake.

* Use about one-third fat to two-thirds mixture, then stir well in a bowl and allow it to set in the container (s). When the mixture has set, gently pull the pot off over the string. Then it's ready to hang up or you turn it out onto your bird table when solid but watch out for squirrels!

You can also feed the birds bread (not stale, and make sure you soak it first), seeds, cooked rice and specially made fat balls bought from garden centres. Then just grab the binoculars and have a little twitching session from the comfort of your kitchen window.

Let's take this outside

Be honest with me, do you actually enjoy staring at a blank wall? Is MTV your channel of choice? Does the smell of stale sweat bring joy to your heart? Thought not, so why do so many of us tolerate it by joining expensive gyms and jostling for position on the step master?

Training outdoors brings with it plenty of benefits, as well as being completely free of charge. For example, outdoor workouts are more challenging because your body has to work harder on uneven surfaces and with the natural elements, and it also improves your balance and core skills. Being outdoors also provides you with essential vitamin D, which helps maintain strong healthy bones and prevent winter blues, and the scenery constantly changes which helps prevent boredom.

But it's too cold out there...

The two main factors that prevent people from exercising outdoors are the weather and safety. Joining an outdoor class such as *British Military Fitness* is a great option as they take safety very seriously and can also provide plenty of tips on how to stay warm, dry and motivated to exercise outdoors all winter long.

If you prefer to go the independent route, remember to layer up, stick to well lit areas if its dark, and tell someone what your planned route is. A bit of advance planning and the right clothing is all it takes to enjoy your outdoor exercise sessions. So still feel like renewing that gym membership? Thought not…

Make do and mend

Jacket absorbing water or tent sprung a leak over the summer? Now is the perfect time to catch up on repairs and save yourself some cash at the same time. There's no need to splash out on new expensive kit (unless of course you want to!) when a few repair tips will easily extend its working life.

Leather boots

Most wear and tear on your leather footwear can be solved, short of an actual hole in the upper. If they're letting in moisture, give them a clean first with a cloth or soft brush and some cleaning product. Then add a waterproofer, making sure to cover all the seams, and allow to dry slowly.

Jackets

If it's torn then you can buy gore-tex patches or puncture kits from outdoor shops, or if your jacket has started to retain moisture rather than repel it, then it just needs reproofing. Give it a clean first with a specialised cleaning product (just pour it in the washing machine tray as normal) then use a reproofing product and follow the directions.

Tents

The best way to prevent damage and leaking is to clean and pack the tent correctly at the end of the season (unless of course you're one of the hardier campers who keeps going year round!).

Give it a sponge down or soak in the bath using a specialised cleaning product, and allow to air dry out of direct sunlight. When it's time to reproof, set the tent up first to make sure the product gets applied to all the nooks and crannies where water could seep in. Some products include a useful UV filter which also protects from sunlight damage over time.

Chase a storm

Weather watching seems to be hardwired into our British psyche. It's one of the few subjects that most of us will happily discuss with perfect strangers, whether it's too wet, too cold, or more rarely, too hot!

So it should come as no surprise that our more extreme weather has spawned a new breed of holiday maker, one who will actually seek out storms, safe in knowledge that they've got a warm, comfortable hotel room to retreat to if it all gets a bit too wild and woolly.

Newquay's Headland Hotel, for example, on Cornwall's rugged Atlantic coast now runs storm-watching weekend-breaks, whilst further north in Scotland, The Banff Springs Hotel and The Corsewall Lighthouse Hotel both offer a grandstand view of the Atlantic storms that blow in.

A less furious but no less dramatic weather phenomenon is the aurora borealis, also known as the Northern Lights. They do make the occasional appearance in British skies, and whilst good displays are fairly uncommon in the UK, your chances certainly improve the further north in Scotland you go and clear frosty nights are thought to be the best time.

Live a 25 hour day

The shorter days of winter are something everyone dreads. Getting up in the dark, and going home in the dark isn't much fun for anyone. Turning the clocks back forces us to switch lights on earlier, costs us more and uses up more carbon.

However the campaign to move the clocks forward permanently has gathered pace in recent years, with The Football Association, England and Wales Cricket Board and Lawn Tennis Association among the organisations pushing the government to change the clocks allowing more time for sport and making society healthier.

According to *The Lighter Later Campaign*, an hour of daylight could be moved from the morning to the evening, when more of us are awake to enjoy it. We'd also save up to 500,000 tons of carbon a year!

Take action

Join the 16,000+ people who have 'liked' the *Lighter Later Campaign* on Facebook, and also email your MP. The more people shout about this issue, the harder it will be for government to ignore.

Bring the outside in

It may be bleak outside, but try one of these little projects to bring some natural colour and beauty into the living room:

✻ Time to redecorate? Take inspiration from a colour in the natural world, take a sample of it e.g a leaf and have a batch of paint made up to match it.

✻ Peel off the carpet or the plaster and reveal the natural wood beneath,

✻ Find lovely rocks to use as doorstops or paperweights.

✻ Grow pumpkins, squashes and gourds, pick them in autumn, dry them out somewhere cool and dark lie a garage or cellar, then wax them and pile them high to display.

✻ Create your own orangerie indoors with dwarf citrus trees. They'll need a light, warm spot with some humidity and they'll will flower all year round indoors as they're self pollinating. If they're happy where they are, they'll start producing fruit around Christmas time.

✻ Brighten up the Christmas table with some paper white narcissi you've grown yourself. Just remember to plant them by mid-November and keep them somewhere cold until the shoots are about 20cm high, them bring them into the warm so they flower in time for the big day.

Grow old disgracefully

Explorer Sir Ranulph Fiennes was 65 when he summited Everest. Entrepreneur Richard Branson attempted to kite surf the Channel for his 60th (though it had to be called off due to adverse weather conditions), and rower Diana Hoff was 55 when she crossed the Atlantic solo.

According to the FAF philosophy, there definitely is no such thing as being 'told old' to have an adventure. Staying active helps to slow the ageing process, and fights off diabetes, heart disease and osteoporosis. So no more excuses, get back on your bike grandpa…

Put your best foot forward

With local authority cuts affecting rights of way departments across the country, just getting out and using your local footpaths will help keep them open and usable for future walkers. You can report any sections that are in need of repair, or any dead ends, to The Ramblers society who want to create a map of the best and worst places to walk in the country.

This information will help them to work with councils to improve the footpath network so that everyone has the opportunity to benefit from walking, wherever they are. There's never been a more important time for us all to do our bit to protect the traditional British Sunday stroll.

Climb a mountain

"It is not the mountain we conquer, but ourselves."
Sir Edmund Hilary

We are not worthy

We may not be the largest country in the world, nor one with the harshest of climates or landscapes, but by God we've produced some world class adventurers. The tough, pioneering, understated kind that always share the glory where it's due, and think nothing of sawing off a couple frostbitten extremities in their garden shed.

Our current crop of explorers and athletes are not only crossing oceans and scaling mountains but also putting the spotlight on key environmental concerns and doing all they can to give something back. An inspiring bunch who might also spur you on to greatness of your own.

Here's a short list of some of my FAF heroes, now if only there was some kind of pin up calendar?...

Bear Grylls – survival expert

Bit controversial this one, as Bear seems to inspire love or hate in people. Perhaps it's because of his high profile on TV and the controversy surrounding the making of his *Born Survivor* shows, but the guy has been doing some seriously inspiring stuff since the tender age of 18.

He was in the SAS for three years, then suffered a broken back following a parachuting accident, only to rally round and become the youngest Briton to climb Everest at age 23. He's gone on to cross the Arctic in an inflatable boat, and the first man to fly over Everest in a paraglider. Nuts? Maybe. Ballsy. Definitely.

Sarah Outen – ocean rower

Back in 2009, 24 year old Sarah Outen completed a 4000 mile epic journey, becoming the first woman to row across the Indian Ocean and the youngest woman to row any ocean for that matter.

She attributes her steely resolve and determination to seeing her own father suffer from arthritis for many years, and teaching her keep going despite life's knockbacks.

She set off again on 1st April 2011 on a solo 20,000-mile trip around the world using nothing more than a kayak, bicycle and rowing boat, to raise money for a variety of causes from breast cancer awareness to WaterAid. She also wanted to fly the flag for women explorers. "It's cool to be spreading the word that women do crazy expeditions too" she said shortly before setting off. "There are a lot of beards in the field."

Ed Stafford – explorer

When Ed Stafford proposed becoming the first person to walk the 4,000-mile length of the Amazon from source to sea, he was roundly dismissed.

Desperate to prove them wrong, the former Army captain set off in April 2008, estimating it would take him a year. Almost two-and-half-years and 859 continuous days of walking later he emerged triumphant from the jungle having contended with vipers, electric eels and even being wrongly accused of murder. The ultimate proof that you should never say never.

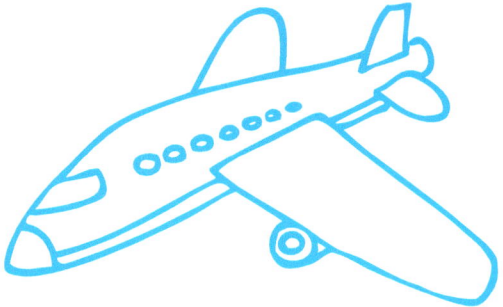

Pen Hadow – arctic explorer and environmentalist

Only one man has ever trekked solo and unsupported to the Geographic North Pole from Canada. Thought to be harder than climbing Everest solo, the feat eluded numerous explorers for 20 years before Pen Hadow came along and in 2003 finally achieved it after 3 previous attempts

.His first hand experience of witnessing worrying changes to the polar ice pushed him to begin working with charities and schools, and he now carries out regular Arctic surveys to bring the world's attention to the plight of the melting ice caps.

Check in at the insect hotel

Insects and invertebrates may not be the prettiest residents of your garden, but they are some of the most useful. These are the guys that will pollinate your plants and gobble up your pests come spring, so it's worth giving them somewhere to hibernate over the winter months, especially in urban areas.

An insect hotel is easy to make. You'll be surprised how many of the materials you already have lying around your home and garden. It will replicate natural features sought by wildlife in your garden - particularly by invertebrates such as ladybirds, as well as frogs, toads and hedgehogs.

In return for building then a winter home, you'll be able to watch a host of different creatures making their homes and learn all about their fascinating behaviour at close quarters.

Design 1

Take a bundle of bamboo canes or other twigs and tie them together with a piece of string. Hang up the bundle under the branch of a tree or to a railing and the bugs will start to move in.

Design 2

Take a plastic drink bottle, cut off the bottom, make holes in the sides and fill with dead leaves after the autumn fall.

Design 3

Take an old plant pot, fill with leaves and turn upside down. It might go against instinct but put it somewhere damp rather than somewhere dry.

Break open the popcorn

It's dark and cold outside, so why not join an armchair expedition and make a journey from summit to sea with one of these hair raising adventure movies and documentaries. Here are a couple of my favourites.

Steep

Lots of jaw dropping footage of big mountain skiing and interviews with the skiers themselves to try and understand what motivates them to take such huge risks in the pursuit of the perfect moment on skis. Inspiring, beautifully shot, and sobering when you learn that two of the skiers profiled died soon after filming ended.

Grizzly man

Follows the life of self-proclaimed kind warrior Timothy Treadwell, a former actor turned wildife preservationist who lived among the grizzlies in a remote section of Alaska for 13 years before eventually dying in a bear attack.

Haunting, touching and complex, a film that stays with you for days afterwards.

Point Break

A more cheerful choice! Yes I realise this one is pure Hollywood rather than documentary, but it has some absolutely classic lines. Who doesn't want to high five Keanu Reeves' character, Johnny Utah when his peeved boss asks him and his partner, "Do either of you have anything even

remotely interesting to tell me?!" and Utah replies "Caught my first tube this morning, sir." Know the feeling, Johnny, know the feeling.

Wake up to a new 9 to 5

According to one survey, 45% of Britons are unhappy in their jobs. Could the answer lie in bringing our professions and passions closer together? If you long to break out of the office and work outdoors, then consider these tips for making a fresh start come the new year…

Look at your work life balance

The daydream of working outdoors could be quite different from the reality. For example, are you ready to invest in retraining or take a pay cut as you work your way up in a new career? Will you have to change location for your new career, and is that practical for your family?

A less radical approach could be to look at your work/life balance. Make more time for your outdoor hobbies. If work is taking over your life then speak to your boss about delegating your workload.

Talk to people who are already doing it

If you're used to office life, then working outdoors will be a complete lifestyle change. Are you ready to be outside in all weathers?

Volunteering is a great to get some hands on experience, or doing a course. Or pick up the phone and offer to shadow someone for a day. Ask questions and get a sense of what it would like on a day to day basis.

Examine what skills you could bring from your old career to your new one

Rather than changing roles, your current job could slot into a new environment. Even adventure companies need accountants, PR officers, HR Managers…

And lastly, it's never too late to make the leap!

Get arty on the beach

Winter is a great time to beach comb as the heavier seas churn up all sorts of treasure. The best time to look is just after high tide, so take a stick for turning things over, a net for catching creatures to look at (but always put them back!) and a bucket for any good finds.

Objects that make great home decorations are frosted fragments of glass in jewel-like colours, colourful string and rope, brightly coloured fishing floats, rusted metal, driftwood and of course, shells. Try arranging them in a bowl or on a shelf, around a candle or glued to a simple picture frame. A few simple ways to bring the seaside closer to home.

Scale a mini Everest

Before they set off for the Himalayas to make their historic attempts on Everest, both Edmund Hilary and George Mallory trained on the slopes of Mount Snowdon. In fact, our British mountain ranges have proved to be a rich training ground for

aspiring mountaineers since the 19th century, when Britain led the boom in recreational mountain climbing (as opposed to climbing mountains for scientific or research purposes).

Our highest peaks are not be sniffed at, with Scafell Pike in the Lake District standing at 978m, Snowdon in North Wales at 1085m and Ben Nevis in Scotland at an impressive 1334m, so if

you have your own dreams of mountaineering glory, Britain is a great place to start.

However, this is a whole different ball game to your average hill walk. Make sure your skills, equipment and fitness are up to the task by signing up for a winter mountaineering course or joining a club.

The British Mountaineering Council
Plas y Brenin The National Mountain Centre

Finally, get your fresh air fix 24/7

Who hasn't dreamed of leaving the city smoke behind and moving closer to the landscape they love, whether it's rolling hills, fresh seaside air or soaring peaks?

Life is too short not to love where you live, and if city life is all getting a bit much then a relocation could be the answer, but how can you be sure it's right for you?

Try before you buy

The National Trust, Landmark Trust and Duchy of Cornwall all have properties on their estates available for holiday rentals, and occasionally for longer tenures. Renting could help you get a feel for an area and whether it would suit you, before having to commit to buying a property.

Ask some honest questions

When researching possible areas to relocate to, be honest about what you're looking for. If you enjoy a busy lifestyle, will there be enough going on locally? If you don't drive, then what are the public transport links like? Also consider how it will affect your job. Will you be commuting or working locally? If so, will there be a demand for your skills in that region, or will you need to retrain? It could the start of a whole new vocation.

Find your own bit of country in the city

If you don't want to abandon city living completely, then there might be ways to make your home feel more like an escape. If your home town or city has a river, then what could be more magical than living on a houseboat, waking up to ducks bobbing up and down out of the window? Or plant a cottage garden or wildflower meadow to transport you back to the countryside every time you step out the back door…

Surrender to the seasons

"Live each season as it passes; breathe the air, drink the drink, taste the fruit, and resign yourself to the influences of each."
Henry David Thoreau

A huge thank you to all my family and friends for all your love and encouragement, and for putting up with my hair brained schemes! This book is dedicated to you.

www.freshairfix.com

www.ingramcontent.com/pod-product-compliance
Lightning Source LLC
Chambersburg PA
CBHW041617220426
43671CB00001B/15